AUSTRALIA

A TRUE BOOK

by
David Petersen

Children's Press®
A Division of Scholastic Inc.

New York Toronto London Auckland Sydney
Mexico City New Delhi Hong Kong
Danbury, Connecticut

Reading Consultant
Linda Cornwell
Learning Resource Consultant
Indiana Department of
Education

A rain forest in
Victoria, Australia

Library of Congress Cataloging-in-Publication Data

Petersen, David, 1946–
    Australia / by David Petersen.
        p.   cm. — (A True book)
    Includes bibliographical references and index.
    Summary: A brief overview of the geography, wildlife, history, and
people of Australia.
    ISBN 0–516–20765–2 (lib. bdg.)   0-516-26372-2 (pbk.)
    1. Australia—Juvenile literature. [1. Australia.] I. Title. II. Series.
DU96.P48 1998
919.4—dc21   97–33041
                                                            CIP
                                                            AC

        13   14   15   R   07   62

Contents

The seasons in Australia are the opposite of those in North America. At this evening Christmas concert in Melbourne, people in the audience wear short sleeves.

Australia—The Land Down Under

The continent of Australia is often called "the land down under." That's because Australia lies in the Southern Hemisphere. You can find it on the bottom half of Earth's globe, below the equator.

In Australia, the seasons are the opposite of those in

North America. Winter comes in June and stays through August. Christmas arrives in the middle of summer!

With a land area of nearly 3 million square miles (8 million square kilometers), Australia is the smallest of the world's seven continents. It is almost as big as the United States, not including Hawaii and Alaska. Yet, Australia has almost 19 million people, while the forty-eight states have more than 279 million!

This picture of Australia, taken high above the earth, shows that much of the continent is covered with brown desert or dry grass-land. The eastern coast receives the most rainfall and is covered in green plants.

The Commonwealth of Australia is a single nation that occupies the entire continent. The Commonwealth consists

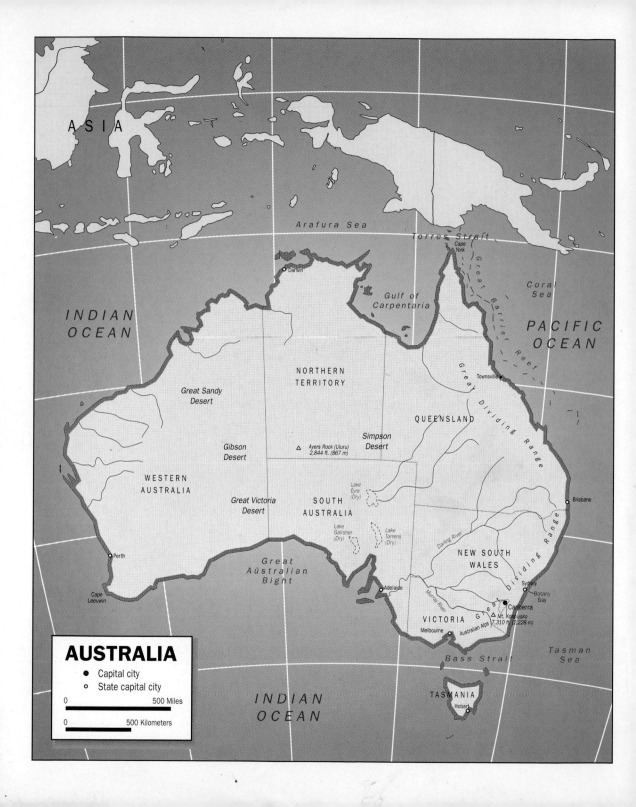

A S I A

Arafura Sea

Torres Strait

Cape
York

*Coral
Sea*

INDIAN
OCEAN

• Darwin

Gulf of
Carpentaria

PACIFIC
OCEAN

*Great Sandy
Desert*

NORTHERN
TERRITORY

Townsville

*Gibson
Desert*

△ Ayers Rock (Uluru)
2,844 ft. (867 m)

*Simpson
Desert*

QUEENSLAND

WESTERN
AUSTRALIA

*Great Victoria
Desert*

SOUTH
AUSTRALIA

*Lake
Eyre
(Dry)*

Brisbane

*Lake
Gairdner
(Dry)*

*Lake
Torrens
(Dry)*

Darling River

NEW SOUTH
WALES

Perth

Cape
Leeuwin

*Great
Australian
Bight*

Adelaide

Murray River

Sydney
Botany
Bay

Canberra
△ Mt. Kosciusko
7,310 ft. (2,228 m)

VICTORIA

Melbourne

Australian Alps

Bass Strait

*Tasman
Sea*

TASMANIA

Hobart

INDIAN
OCEAN

AUSTRALIA

- ● Capital city
- ○ State capital city

0   500 Miles

0   500 Kilometers

of six states: New South Wales, Victoria, Queensland, South Australia, Western Australia, and Tasmania.

Australia is surrounded by water, making it the only island continent. If you go wading on Australia's eastern sea coast, you'll be wetting your toes in the South Pacific Ocean. If you go swimming on Australia's west coast, you'll be splashing in the Indian Ocean.

Most Australians live in the east, along the Pacific seacoast. The Pacific seacoast is cooler and gets more rain than the rest of the continent. The country's two largest cities—

Australia is surrounded by water on all sides. Going to the beach is a popular pastime.

Melbourne, in southeastern Australia, is the continent's second-largest city.

Sydney and Melbourne—are both in far eastern Australia. The capital city, Canberra, is also on the east coast.

The Outback

Australians call the vast area in the middle of their continent the "outback." Much of the outback is desert—dry, treeless, and hot. There are no cities there, and very few people.

There is little water in the outback. Most of the rivers and lakes are dry much of the time.

Much of the outback is hot, dry desert.

Underground water is plentiful but too salty for people to drink or for watering crops.

However, cattle and sheep can drink the salty water. They can also graze on the grasses and

Many areas of the outback that are not desert are used for raising cattle (above). Few people live in the outback. Small, rugged cafes such as this one (right) serve the few people who do live there.

shrubs that grow in parts of the outback. Raising cattle and sheep is now Australia's biggest business.

Flat as a Cracker

Most of Australia is "flat as a cracker," but it does have some mountainous areas. The highest point on the continent is Mount Kosciusko, rising 7,310 feet (2,228 meters) above the near-by Pacific Ocean.

Water from rain and melting snow rushes down from the

These skiers (left) are on Mount Kosciusko, Australia's highest point. The Murray River (below) is Australia's longest permanent river.

coastal mountains to feed the nation's longest permanent river, the Murray. After winding west across Australia for 1,609 miles (2,589 km), the Murray

River empties into the Indian Ocean.

The country's lowest point is Lake Eyre, deep in the outback. It sits 52 feet (16 m) below sea level and is usually just a dry bed of salt. Water runs into the lake only after heavy rains.

Perth, on Australia's west coast, is the continent's only major city not in the east.

A coral reef is made of the skeletons of billions of tiny sea creatures. It lies just under—or just above—the ocean surface. Australia's Great Barrier Reef is the world's largest coral formation.

The Great Barrier Reef actually consists of 2,500 small reefs and islands. It stretches 1,250 miles (2,010 km) along Australia's northeastern coast. This reef is the largest structure ever made by living creatures. It is visible from the moon!

Looking down into the clear water, the bright colors and strange shapes of the giant coral castles are dazzling. And this gorgeous underwater world is home to millions of glittering fish.

Tasmania

Off the southern tip of Australia lies the island of Tasmania. Although 150 miles (240 km) of ocean separates Tasmania from the rest of Australia, it is con-sidered part of the continent.

Long ago, Tasmania was attached to the mainland like a toe. Then, about twelve

Hobart is the capital of Tasmania and the state's largest city.

thousand years ago, the sea rose, covering a section of land that joined Tasmania to the rest of the continent.

Unlike the dry, flat outback, Tasmania is wet, cool, mountain-

Tasmania is cool, mountainous, and rainy. Pictured above is Lake Dove. Pictured to the right is Russell Falls in Tasmania's Mount Field National Park.

ous, and green. A bush growing there, called Kings Holly, may be the Earth's oldest living thing. Scientists believe it has survived continuously for more than forty thousand years!

Strange Wildlife

Australia became separated from the other continents about 200 million years ago. As a result, its plants and animals have become very different from those in other parts of the world.

You probably know what a kangaroo looks like. It resem-

Kangaroos carry their young in a pouch on their stomach. A baby kangaroo is called a joey.

bles a giant rabbit and hops about on its big back legs.

Another well-known Australian animal is the koala. It looks like a teddy bear, with a small, furry body and big, sleepy eyes. But koalas are not really bears. Koalas live in eucalyptus trees and eat eucalyptus leaves.

Kangaroos and koalas are members of a large group of animals, called mammals, that nurse their young on mother's milk. Being a mammal is not unusual. Dogs and cats are mammals, and so are people. But kangaroos and koalas belong to a rare group of mammals called marsupials.

Newborn marsupials are very tiny. For example, a newborn

The koala is another marsupial that lives in Australia.

kangaroo is only 1 inch (2.5 centimeters) long. In this group of animals, the mother carries her baby around in a pouch on her stomach. Inside the pouch, the baby marsupial rides in safety and comfort and nurses whenever it wants. The baby leaves when it's big enough to find food on it's own.

Almost all of the world's marsupials live in Australia. There's the beaver-like wombat, the cat-like Tasmanian devil, the dog-like Tasmanian wolf, and well over a hundred more.

More rare than marsupials are Australia's three species of monotremes, or egg-laying mammals. The strangest of all is the platypus. This shy, furry

creature is about as big as a cat. It lives in water and uses its webbed feet and a paddle-like tail for swimming. It gets its nickname "duck-bill" from its long, flat bill.

The strange-looking platypus (above) is one of the few kinds of mammals that lays eggs. Australia is home to many colorful birds, including these rainbow lorikeets (right).

Australia also has many familiar animals, including snakes, crocodiles, and hundreds of species of birds.

Discovery

In 1606, the Spanish explorer Willem Jansz became the first European to see Australia, getting only a distant view as his ship sailed by. A few years later, Dutch explorers sailed around the island continent and briefly explored the land.

In 1770, Captain James Cook of the British Navy explored Australia's Pacific coast. Captain Cook claimed the continent for England.

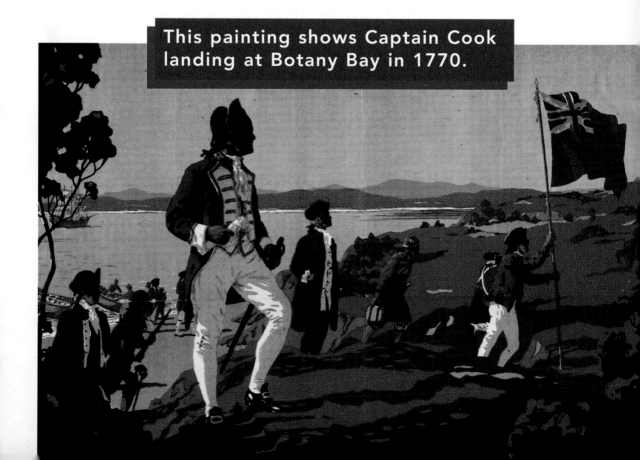

This painting shows Captain Cook landing at Botany Bay in 1770.

At first, Australia was considered worthless. Most of the land was not good for farming. However, England's prisons were overcrowded, so the English government decided to send some convicted criminals to faraway Australia.

In January 1788, about 730 convicts and their guards landed at Botany Bay on Australia's Pacific coast. The town they built there would grow to become Sydney, Australia's largest city.

In less than a century, 160,000 criminals were brought to the land down under. A few free settlers came too, but Australia's European population grew slowly. By 1850, there were only about 400,000 white residents.

Then, in 1851, gold was discovered and Europeans came by the thousands. When the gold rush fizzled out ten years later, the

Europeans traveled to Australia in large numbers after gold was discovered there in 1851.

country's white population had almost tripled. The European population has steadily increased ever since.

The First People

Europeans were not the first people to live in Australia. At least forty thousand years before Captain Cook arrived, other people had made the continent their home. These first people came from Southeast Asia in rafts and canoes, traveling from island to island.

Aborigine dancers

The dark-skinned descendants of these early explorers are known today as Aborigines. Aborigine means "native."

For thousands of years, the Aborigine people were Australia's only human inhabitants. They lived by hunting and by gathering plants. An important Aborigine hunting weapon is a special throwing stick called a boomerang. Some boomerangs are made so that they circled back to the thrower, but these usually were not used for hunting.

Australia's native people were almost wiped out by European settlers. Many died of diseases brought by the newcomers. Many starved to death when their land was stolen. Many others were murdered.

Aborigine children in school (above). An Aborigine man carves a boomerang (right).

In 1770, when Captain Cook arrived, Australia was home to about 400,000 Aborigines. In 1870, there were only 60,000.

Today, Aborigines number more than 250,000, and they are Australian citizens with the

The Australian government is trying to bring Australia's many peoples closer together. This mosaic in front of the New Parliament House in Canberra was designed by artist Michael Tjakamarra Nelson, an Aborigine. The design is based on traditional Aborigine sand paintings.

same rights as other Australians. Problems remain, but the country is making amends for its past mistreatment of Australia's first citizens.

Uluru

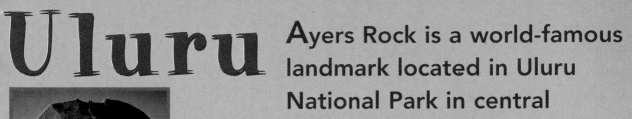

Ayers Rock is a world-famous landmark located in Uluru National Park in central Australia. This huge, red rock formation is 1.5 miles (2.4 km) long. It rises 1,142 feet (348 m) above the desert and 2,844 feet (867m) above sea level. It is visible for miles in every direction. Ayers Rock is called Uluru by Australia's native people. To them, it is a sacred place. In Uluru's caves, many walls are covered with beautiful and mysterious paintings made long ago by Aborigine artists.

Australia Today and Tomorrow

On January 1, 1901, Australia won its independence from Britain, becoming the Commonwealth of Australia. Australians still honor the queen of England as their monarch, but their political leader is a prime minister elected by the people.

Sydney is Australia's largest city. The shell-like Sydney Opera House in the foreground is the city's most famous landmark.

Australia is a vast, sun-drenched land of deserts, coral reefs, and sandy beaches. The continent is home to many kinds of animals including cattle, sheep, kangaroos, and koalas.

Most Australians are fond of the outdoors. Left, a family hikes in the Australian Alps in the southeast. This large celebration (right) on New Year's Eve in 1996 was part of Australia's preparation for the 2000 Summer Olympics, which was held in Sydney.

Australia may be "down under" geographically, but it's near the top in international respect. And its future is expected to be as sunny as its weather.

Australia Fast Facts

Area 2,967,909 square miles
(7,686,850 sq. km), including Tasmania

Highest point Mount Kosciusko, 7,310 feet
(2,228 m) above sea level

Lowest point Lake Eyre, 52 feet (16 m)
below sea level

Longest Permanent River Murray
1,609 miles (2,589 km)

Capital Canberra

Population 18,972,350

To Find Out More

Here are some additional resources to help you learn more about the continent of Australia:

Books

Allison, R. J. **Australia.** Raintree Steck-Vaughn, 1996.

Darian-Smith, Kate. **Australia and Oceania.** Raintree Steck-Vaughn, 1997.

Darian-Smith, Kate. **Exploration into Australia.** New Discovery Books, 1996.

Darian-Smith, Kate, and David Lowe. **The Australian Outback and Its People.** Thomson Learning, 1995.

Lowe, David and Andrea Shimmen. **Australia.** Raintree Steck-Vaughn, 1997.

Preller, James. **In Search of the Real Tasmanian Devil.** Scholastic, 1996.

Seibert, Patricia. **Toad Overload: A True Tale of Nature Knocked Off Balance in Australia.** Millbrook Press, 1995.

Short, Joan. **Platypus.** Mondo, 1997.

Tesar, Jenny E. **What on Earth is a Quokka?** Blackbirch Press, 1997.

Twist, Clint. **James Cook Across the Pacific to Australia.** Raintree Steck-Vaughn, 1995.

Organizations and Online Sites

Bushrangers
http://scs.une.edu.au/Bush rangers/home.htm

This site helps you learn about the exciting early history of colonial Australia.

Council for Aboriginal Reconciliation
http://www.austlii.edu.au/ au/orgs/car

Dedicated to improving the relationship between Aborigines and the rest of Australia's inhabitants. Tries to find ways to make up for past crimes against Aborigines.

INTELLiCast: Australia Weather
http://www.intellicast.com

Forecasts and weather information for Australia.

Didjeridu Australia
http://www.didgeridoo-australia.com/home.htm

Look at pictures of Australia's native animals and plants.

The Travel Assistant
http://www.travelassistant. com.au/

This guide to Australia features lots of photos and descriptions of the continent's landmarks.

Important Words

Australia from the Latin word australis, meaning "southern"

continent one of the seven large land masses of the earth

convict a person found guilty of a crime

equator an imaginary line around the center of the world's globe

geography the study of Earth's continents, oceans, and other physical features

graze to feed on

monarch ruler of a kingdom or empire; king or queen

permanent river a river that is never dry

Southern Hemisphere the bottom half of the world's globe

species a distinct kind of animal or plant

Index

Meet the Author

As a pilot in the U.S. Marine Corps, David Petersen traveled widely. Today, he lives with his lovely wife, Caroline, in a little cabin on a big mountain in Colorado. He enjoys reading, writing, and walking his dogs in the forest. His most recent "big people" book is *Ghost Grizzlies: Does the Great Bear Still Haunt Colorado?* (Henry Holt & Co.) Mr. Petersen has written many other books on geography for Children's Press, including True Books on all the continents.